SESAME STREET

Everyone Has VALUE with Zoe

A Book about Respect

Marie-Therese Miller

Lerner Publications ◆ Minneapolis

Sesame Street's mission has always been about teaching kids much more than simply the ABCs and 123s. This series of books about nurturing the positive character traits of generosity, respect, empathy, positive thinking, resilience, and persistence will help children grow into the best versions of themselves. So come along with your funny, furry friends from Sesame Street as they learn about making themselves—and the world—smarter, stronger, and kinder.

—**Sincerely, the Editors at Sesame Street**

TABLE OF CONTENTS

What Is Respect?

Respect means treating other people the way you want to be treated.

Showing Respect

Show respect when your friends talk.

Use kind words when you speak.

Say *please* and *thank you*.

Act with respect.

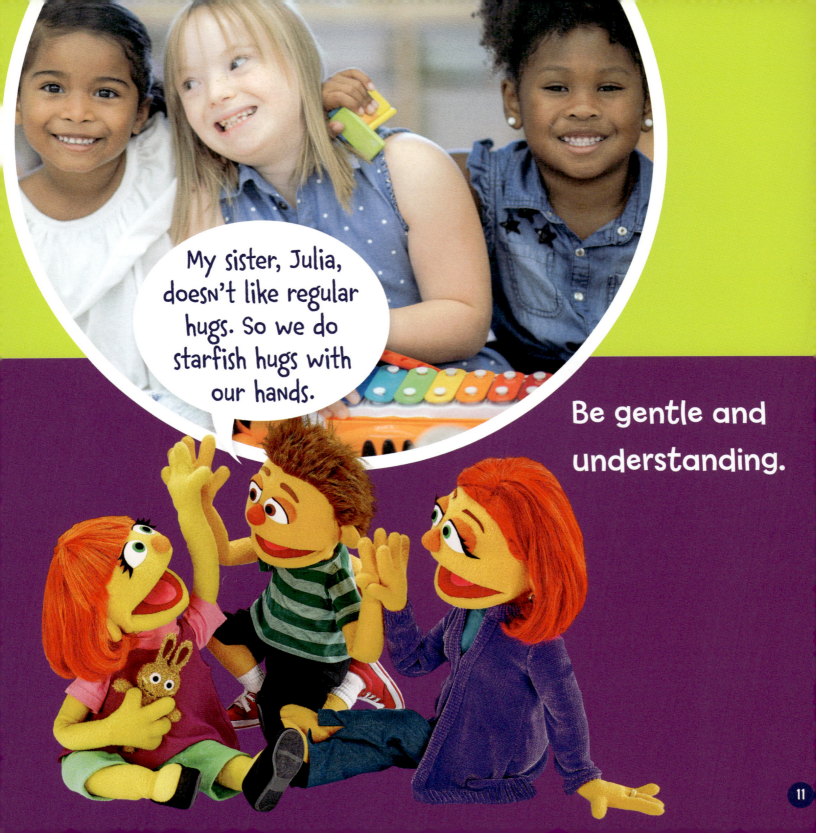

My sister, Julia, doesn't like regular hugs. So we do starfish hugs with our hands.

Be gentle and understanding.

People might do things
differently from you.

How can you respect someone who does things differently?

They deserve your respect.

13

People might have different ideas than you do.

Bert and I don't always agree. He is still my buddy.

They deserve your respect too.

Follow the rules at school and at home.

Why do you think it's important to respect your teachers and parents?

Respect your belongings.

Take good care of toys and books.

I keep my fairy tale books sparkling!

Choose healthy foods. Sleep well and exercise. Treat everyone with respect, including yourself!

How else can you respect yourself?

BE A BUDDY!

Put on a play with a friend. Imagine you are a teacher and your friend is a new student in your classroom. Your characters are showing each other respect. How are you showing respect? How are you speaking with respect? Act it out!

Glossary

belongings: things that are yours

differently: not in the same way

exercise: to move your body

idea: a thought or opinion

sparkling: shining

understanding: kind and accepting

Learn More

Miller, Marie-Therese. *Caring with Bert and Ernie: A Book about Empathy.* Minneapolis: Lerner Publications, 2021.

Miller, Pat Zietlow. *Be Kind.* New York: Roaring Brook, 2018.

Murphy, Frank. *Stand Up for Respect.* Ann Arbor, MI: Cherry Lake, 2019.

Index

Photo Acknowledgments

Additional Image credits: monkeybusinessimages/Getty Images, p. 4; WhitneyLewisPhotography/Getty Images, p. 5; Yakobchuk Viacheslav/Shutterstock.com, p. 6; Cavan Images/Getty Images, p. 7; wavebreakmedia/Shutterstock.com, p. 8; fizkes/Shutterstock.com, p. 9; Robert Kneschke/EyeEm/Getty Images, p. 10; FatCamera/E+/Getty Images, pp. 11–12; Lavi Dhurve/EyeEm/Getty Images, p. 13; Monkey Business Images/Shutterstock.com, p. 14; Elyas Bakri/EyeEm/Getty Images, p. 15; Jose Luis Pelaez Inc/DigitalVision/Getty Images, p. 16; SDI Productions/E+/Getty Images, p. 17; kate_sept2004/E+/Getty Images, p. 18; MoMo Productions/DigitalVision/Getty Images, p. 19; Sasi Ponchaisang/EyeEm/Getty Images, p. 20.

For my family of Sesame Street enthusiasts:
John E., Michelle, Meghan, John Vincent, Erin, Elizabeth, and Greyson

Lerner Publications Company
An imprint of Lerner Publishing Group, Inc.
241 First Avenue North
Minneapolis, MN 55401 USA

For reading levels and more information, look up this title at www.lernerbooks.com.

Main body text set in Billy Infant. Typeface provided by SparkyType.

Editor: Alison Lorenz **Designer:** Emily Harris **Photo Editor:** Brianna Kaiser

Library of Congress Cataloging-in-Publication Data

Names: Miller, Marie-Therese, 1960- author.
Title: Everyone Has Value with Zoe: a book about respect / Marie-Therese Miller.
Description: Minneapolis : Lerner Publications, 2021 | Series: Sesame Street character guides | Includes bibliographical references and index. | Audience: Ages 4–8 | Audience: Grades K–1 | Summary: "What does respect look like? With help from their Sesame Street friends, young readers learn how they can respect their parents, their teachers, and themselves"— Provided by publisher.
Identifiers: LCCN 2020003375 (print) | LCCN 2020003376 (ebook) | ISBN 9781728403939 (library binding) | ISBN 9781728418759 (ebook)
Subjects: LCSH: Respect for persons—Juvenile literature. | Respect—Juvenile literature.
Classification: LCC BJ1533.R42 M55 2021 (print) | LCC BJ1533.R42 (ebook) | DDC 179/.9—dc23

LC record available at https://lccn.loc.gov/2020003375
LC ebook record available at https://lccn.loc.gov/2020003376

Manufactured in the United States of America
1-48393-48907-5/4/2020